ADVENTURES RISK IN URUGUAY

Linda A. de Gonzalez

BEACON HILL PRESS OF KANSAS CITY
Kansas City, Missouri

Copyright 1983, 1986, 1991, 1996
By Beacon Hill Press of Kansas City
Fourth Edition 1996
ISBN 083-410-8186

Printed in the
United States of America

Cover design: Mike Walsh
Illustration by: Keith Alexander

All Scripture quotations are taken from the *Holy Bible, New International Version*® (NIV®). Copyright © 1973, 1978, 1984 by International Bible Society. Used by permission of Zondervan Publishing House. All rights reserved.

Permission to quote from the following copyrighted version of the Bible is also acknowledged with appreciation:

The Living Bible (TLB), © 1971. Used by permission of Tyndale House Publishers, Inc., Wheaton, IL 60189. All rights reserved.

Note: This book is part of the Children's Mission Education Curriculum. It is designed for use in Year 1, Culture. This year examines the ways different groups of people live and the challenges the cultures present missionaries. This book was chosen for use in this year because it supports these purposes. The people and incidents contained in this book are real; however, conversation and detail consistent with the times have been added.

10   9   8   7   6   5   4   3   2   1

Dedicated to

My parents, Jack and Janet Armstrong, who included me in their missionary calling and taught me as a child what serving God is really all about

and to

my husband, Daniel Gonzalez, who shared his homeland with me and who has given me the privilege of serving God in our beloved Uruguay

Contents

Preface	7
1. A Lucky MK	9
2. A Very Long Trip	14
3. New Friends in a New Country	20
Mabel	22
Daniel	25
4. A Very Different School	29
5. Gauchos and Holidays	34
Holiday Quiz	34
Recipe for Torta Frita	36
Bible Story Quiz	38
6. My Favorite Holiday: Christmas	40
Postscript	45

Preface

You will probably meet many missionaries as you attend the Church of the Nazarene. They will share many new and interesting things about their countries.

Through this book, I'd like to share my experience and feelings as the child of missionaries.

I would also like to tell you about the exciting country of Uruguay, from a child's point of view, so you will be able to see the similarities and differences between your home and mine.

May God bless you as you read, and teach you how you, too, can serve Him as a child!

Sincerely,
LINDA A. DE GONZALEZ

1

A Lucky MK

Hi! My name is Linda. I'm an MK (missionaries' kid). I live in South America. My life is full of adventures. I travel to faraway countries and learn new languages. I go to school with boys and girls from all over the world. My family is very international. My dad was born in London, England. My mother was born in Pennsylvania. I was born in Bolivia, South America. I have a younger sister, Beverly, who was born in Uruguay (YOUR-a-goo-ay).

At home we speak English. We live like most other families back home. But at school, church, and in the neighborhood, we speak Spanish. I eat many different kinds of foods, like chorizo (choe-REE-sews) and asado (as-SAH-doe). Once every four years I travel to the United States. I get to visit my grandparents and fill up on chocolate milkshakes and cheeseburgers.

My parents love the Lord and serve Him in many ways. They preach and teach in the Bible school. They build churches and teach Sunday School classes.

When I was three years old, my parents went "home on furlough." This means they returned to the United States for a year of rest. It didn't seem to me that my dad got much rest. He was so busy. I didn't see him very much for several months. He traveled across the United States and Canada, preaching and showing slides about Nazarene missionary work in Bolivia.

Sometimes my mother and I went with him. It was very exciting. My mother would dress me up like a Bolivian Indian. I would wear a long, gathered, red velvet skirt and a shiny turquoise blouse. I rolled my baby doll up in a bright striped shawl tied around my shoulders and carried her on my back. I braided my hair and wore my black felt hat. It was frightening to stand up on the platform in front of a full church. But I felt very important when my dad would ask me to help him sing in Aymara, the language most of the Indians speak in La Paz (lah PAHTH).

I loved living with my grandparents that year. Mother says they spoiled me. But you see, the only time I get to visit my relatives is when we are "on furlough." My grandma made up for all of those years. That is only once every four years. She read hundreds of bedtime stories to me and kept the freezer full of ice cream. My grandpa took me shopping. Even though he was a dentist, he bought me many candy bars!

One of the best trips we took that year was a train ride to Toronto, Canada. There I met my other grandparents and several aunts, uncles, and cousins. I recognized my grandparents, because I'd seen their picture many times. I finally got to meet an aunt who'd sent me nice birthday presents. Most of all I enjoyed playing with my cousins. They taught me how to build a snowman, and we had a great snowball fight. I watched them ice-skate. It looked so easy, I decided to try it. But my ankles were so wobbly I kept falling down.

One day my dad came home with the most won-

derful news! Our year of furlough was over, and we would be moving to a new country called Uruguay. Mother took out our map of South America and helped me find it. First, she pointed to Brazil, the biggest country. Then she showed me a little triangle just below Brazil. That's Uruguay! Can you find it on the map?

Daddy said we would be moving to the capital city, Montevideo (mon-tay-vee-DAY-oh). I was really excited to see it was on the coast. That meant I could get a new bathing suit. I hoped to do a lot of swimming at the beach. Dad started to dream about an outboard motor. He got all of his fishing gear ready.

Mother and I were very busy making plans. We would be gone for five years. Since clothes are expensive in Uruguay, we made a list of things to buy. A lady from the church took us shopping. She bought me three winter coats. Each one was a different size, so I could grow into it. The ladies in another Sunday School class surprised me. They bought five beautiful Sunday dresses and five school dresses. The missionary society gave me several pairs of shoes, in different colors and sizes. It was more exciting than Christmas! Oh, yes, I went shopping for toys too. Mother let me choose my favorite ones, and then she bought some to put away until I grew up a little.

My dad was worried because he wasn't sure how to pack everything. We kept giving him more things—sheets, towels, dishes, pots and pans, electrical appliances, clothes, toys, and our washer and dryer.

I will never forget the last church service in our home church. It was a special "send-off" service. Have you ever been to one? My family sat up front on the platform. The pastor told us that the whole church would be praying for us. Then several people stood up and read some wonderful promises from God's Word. They let us know that even though we would be living far away, God would take care of us. One of my favorite promises is Deuteronomy 31:8, "Don't be afraid, for the Lord will go before you and will be with you; he will not fail nor forsake you" (TLB).

We sang our favorite hymns and closed with a beautiful prayer. I realized then that I was a missionary too. I had to tell the boys and girls in Uruguay about Jesus. I prayed that God would help me.

2

A Very Long Trip

Dad showed me on the map that Montevideo was over 8,000 miles away. I had no idea how far that was until we got on the airplane and started flying south. It took us all day, all night, and part of the next day to get there.

At first I was very excited. I got the window seat and watched the city grow smaller until it disappeared. For a while I studied the clouds. I imagined I saw giant white bears, sailboats, and ice cream cones. But as we climbed higher and higher, we left the clouds far below.

I was getting tired of looking out into empty blue space. Then the stewardess came by. She offered us soft drinks and promised to return in a few minutes with supper. Supper was served in fancy little dishes. I managed to eat it all without spilling anything!

Just as I was finishing my dessert the pilot spoke to us over the loudspeaker. He said that we would soon begin to descend and would be landing in Miami in about half an hour.

For one terrible moment I thought we'd gotten on the wrong plane! Mother laughed. She explained

that Montevideo was so far away we would be landing in several cities along the way. That was so the plane could refuel and pick up new passengers.

Each time we boarded the plane I faced a new challenge. The first one was saying good-bye to my grandparents. When I thought about waiting five years to see them again, my eyes filled up with tears. I really tried hard not to cry. "Dear God," I prayed, "please help me to be brave!"

When we reboarded the plane in Miami I thought we had made another mistake. It seemed that everybody was talking nonsense. I couldn't understand a thing anyone said. Even the stewardess talked funny. I wondered if I would ever be able to talk to people in such a strange-sounding language! I was really glad that God understood English.

Across the aisle I saw a little girl who looked scared. When I smiled at her, she smiled back. "Hi, my name is Linda. What's yours?" I asked politely.

But she only smiled back. Mother explained that she probably didn't speak English. Mother began to teach me how to say some words in Spanish. I practiced a few times. Then I looked over at the little girl and repeated my question in Spanish.

To my surprise, she understood. She rattled off a very long name, which I didn't catch. I was excited! Maybe I could learn Spanish after all. Mother had been making me a picture dictionary. She decided it was time I tried to use it. It looked something like this:

yo (yoh)—me
papa (pah-PAH)—father
abuela (ah-boo-AY-lah)—grandma
nina (NEEN-yah)—girl
la iglesia (lah ee-GLAY-see-ah)—the church
la casa (lah CAH-sah)—the house
mama (mah-MAH)—mother
bebe (bay-BAY)—baby
abuelo (ah-boo-AY-low)—grandpa
nino (NEEN-yoh)—boy
la escuela (lah es-QUAY-lah)—the school
la tienda (lah TEE-end-ah)—the store
vamos a (VAH-mohs ah)—let's go, or let's go to
jugar (hoo-GAR)—play

yo (yoh) me

mama (mah-MAH) mother

papa (pah-PAH) father

bebe (bay-BAY) baby

abuela (ah-boo-AY-lah) grandma

abuelo (ah-boo AY-low) grandpa

nina (NEE-neeah) girl

nino (NEE-neeoh) boy

la iglesia (lah ee-GLAY-see-ah) the church

la escuela (lah es-QUAY-lay) the school

la casa (lah CAH-sah) the house

la tienda (lah TEE-end-ah) the store

vamos a (VAH-mohs ah) let's go, or let's go to

jugar (hoo-GAR) play

leer (lay-HEIR) read

dormir (thor-MEER) sleep

orar (oh-RARE) pray

mirar t.v. (mee-RARE tay-vay) watch T.V.

17

leer (lay-HEIR)—read
dormir (thor-MEER)—sleep
orar (oh-RARE)—pray
mirar TV (mee-RARE tay-vay)—watch TV

    I shared my picture dictionary with the little girl. It was like a game. I taught her how to say the words in English. She taught me how to say the words in Spanish. We laughed at each other because it all sounded so strange. But between the giggles, I was learning Spanish!

    Have you ever tried to learn another language? It's a lot easier if you have a friend to teach you. A picture dictionary is a fun way to start too. You can cut pictures out of magazines or draw them yourself. Your friend can teach you how to say each word. You can teach your friend English. Try it! You may want to copy these words to get you started in Spanish. A tape recorder really helps too. It will help you remember the right way to say each word. Remember to laugh a lot in between!

    This trip was certainly getting interesting. Our next stop was Buenos Aires, Argentina. I could hardly believe it when the pilot told us to put on our winter coats. It was only 40 degrees outside! This was August! When we were in Miami it had been too hot to wear a sweater. Now we were in the middle of winter. Dad had warned me about the changes in climate. He said that after we crossed the equator everything would be the opposite. But I hadn't really believed it would change so much.

    There was another big difference too. We landed at night. I looked up at the sky. It didn't look right. The moon was the same, but the stars seemed to twinkle differently. Do you know why? From the Southern

Hemisphere, you can't see all of the stars that you see in the north. I searched and searched for the Big Dipper and the North Star. But instead, I kept seeing a cross. Mother explained that the cross was called the Southern Cross. It is the most famous constellation in the Southern Hemisphere.

Changes in language, changes in weather, changes in the sky, making new friends, and leaving relatives behind—Uruguay was certainly a long, long way from home!

3

New Friends in a New Country

The flight across the river to Montevideo took less than an hour. After 24 hours of traveling, we were finally in Uruguay. Suddenly I became very scared! I tried to hide behind Mother as we walked down the ramp toward the airport. But I was so curious, I peeked to see what was next. The balcony was full of people. Everyone was waving and smiling and shouting at once.

Then I heard a man's voice shout: "Hi, Linda! Welcome to Uruguay!" I peeked again and saw three or four American kids almost falling over the railing, waving and smiling at me! I was excited and embarrassed at the same time. I waved and then ducked behind Mother's red coat. It seemed like the whole airport was full of Nazarenes. Everyone seemed to be greeting us at once. I had so many mixed-up feelings. I felt happy, tired, excited, worried, proud, curious, and shy all at the same time.

We had to go through some offices and customs. There a guard opened all of our suitcases and checked

to make sure we weren't bringing in illegal goods. I checked to make sure he didn't take any of the candy bars Grandpa had tucked in at the last minute.

Finally, we walked through the big glass door and were surrounded by new friends. Everyone was talking in Spanish. One by one they came over and kissed me! In Uruguay, people always give each other a kiss on the cheek when they meet. Mother and Daddy looked as surprised as I.

Suddenly a little girl came over and said in perfect English, "Hi! I'm Marsha Denton. I hope we can be very good friends." I recognized her as one of the kids who had been yelling over the balcony. "Here are my two brothers, Ronnie and Danny. We've been waiting to see you."

Marsha's parents became my new aunt and uncle. You see, on a mission field each missionary family adopts each other and forms a new family. Since we live too far away to see our real aunts and uncles, we adopt missionary aunts, uncles, and cousins. We celebrate all holidays and birthdays together, like a real family.

We finally arrived at our new house, where Aunt Ruth and Aunt Sarah had fixed a delicious supper.

As I got into bed that night, I had a lot to thank God for: a safe trip, a beautiful house, a new family, and a wonderful friend, Marsha. But most of all I thanked God for my new home country—Uruguay!

My parents were assigned to pastor the Nazarene church in Carrasco. It is a pretty neighborhood on the outskirts of the city. The church rented a little hall where they held services. It was there that I really learned to speak and understand Spanish. It was fun to listen as the boys and girls sang choruses in Spanish. I had sung many of them in Sunday School in English. I quickly learned to join in. I also made a lot of new friends. I'd like to introduce you to my two best Uruguayan friends. They will tell you a little about themselves.

Mabel (mah-BELL)

I am glad that Linda's parents came to pastor my church, because I was looking for a Christian friend.

Linda and I love bike riding. We have fun riding around the neighborhood.

When Linda comes to spend the night at my house, we stay up late and talk. We get up real early in the morning. I have to run errands for my mother before breakfast. Each morning I must go buy fresh milk and rolls. Linda thinks it's strange we don't eat eggs or cereal. I'm teaching her that the best thing for breakfast is a good hot cup of "cafe con leche" (hot milk with coffee flavoring) and a couple of fresh rolls from the bakery.

She's teaching me English, while I teach her Spanish. You should hear the funny mistakes we make! One day I asked for some "soup and water" to wash my hands.

What I like best of all is the Bible club we've started in my backyard. We sing, memorize scripture, and listen to Bible stories. I love to teach. Linda says she is going to be a teacher when she grows up, so we have fun practicing on our friends. We are sharing Jesus' love with many of my neighbors who don't know who Jesus is.

I'm looking forward to teaching Sunday School someday. But for now I pay close attention to what Mrs. Armstrong teaches. You see, I have a lot to learn about the Bible. My mother and I just started going to church two years ago. We are learning about Jesus together.

My dad does not go to church at all. Neither do most of the men I know. Dad says that church is for women and children. I don't think that's so. But for now all I can do is pray that God will change his mind. Then maybe someday we can all go to church together.

Last year I asked Jesus to forgive my sins. One of

the first things I want to do when I'm 12 years old is get baptized. The second thing I want to do is find someone who will let me teach Sunday School.

When I am old enough to earn some money, I want to visit the United States. I want to see all of the strange and wonderful things Linda tells me about. In the meantime, I'm teaching her all about Uruguay.

We took a bus downtown last week, and I showed her the legislative palace. It is like the U.S. Capitol in Washington, D.C. I also showed her our president's house. We watched the changing of the guard by the statue of Artigas (are-TEA-gahs). He's our national hero. We saw the monument to our flag. It is striped in light blue and white, the colors of the sky. In the corner, instead of stars, we have a big, bright, smiling yellow sun. It is the symbol of hope for a new day of freedom, peace, and prosperity. Linda told me it is sort of like her American flag.

I'm really glad Linda came to Uruguay. I believe God has many wonderful things for us to learn together.

Daniel

Hi! My name is Daniel Gonzalez. I'm one of Linda's best church friends. I was born and raised in Montevideo. One day I was playing cowboys and Indians on the sidewalk. A missionary interrupted our game. He rode a motorcycle down our street. He used a loudspeaker to announce that a new church was coming to our neighborhood. When he saw my friends and me, he smiled and said, "We have very special things for boys and girls. Be sure to come this Sunday morning at ten o'clock. I will give each of you a balloon as an extra treat. Don't miss this one and only chance! Come and get your free balloon!" Then he rode away.

My friends and I were excited. There was no church in our neighborhood. But the man on the motorcycle had looked friendly and had told us about stories and crafts and songs. It sounded like fun! I knew I was going for sure when the man said we could have a balloon!

Boy, am I glad I went! I had never seen anything like it before. The neatest thing of all were the stories he told. He told us about a guy called Daniel. That made me really sit still and listen. I didn't know very much about God. I wondered if such a story could be true. I was afraid to ask my dad about it. He never went to any church. He didn't know very much about God either.

The only person that seemed to know about God was the missionary. I decided to go to Sunday School every week and find out if these things were really true. But on Sunday mornings there are lots of other fun things to do. Sometimes I'd get involved in a soccer game and forget all about church. My friends and I would chase birds with our slingshots. On cold, rainy days, I'd usually sleep in. On warm, sunny days, my family would go to the beach.

But as the months went by, I became more and more interested in Sunday School. My older sister, Susana, started to attend every week. She would remind me to get up early and run my errands so I could go to church. Everyone in my family had a job to do. Mine was to go to the store and buy fresh milk every morning for breakfast. Susana had to make all the beds and sweep the room. Ed, my brother, went to the bakery for fresh bread.

I became a Christian after I attended Boys' and Girls' Camp. I'll never forget that camp! I'd never gone camping before. It was quite an adventure! Fifty boys and girls from different Nazarene churches piled into a bus, and we took off. I'd never been out of Montevideo. So I sat by the window to get a good look at my country.

We rode through the rolling hills and vast meadows. We saw several peach and apple orchards, vineyards, and a few chicken farms. But mostly we saw sheep and cattle grazing in the wide open fields.

As a matter of fact, our camp was held in the middle of a grazing field. There was one very large brown tent, which was our dining room and indoor chapel. There were two big white tents to sleep in. One was for boys and the other was for girls.

I was really glad my bunk was on the bottom. One day a big tarantula climbed across our tent's ceiling, right above my bed. The boy who slept on the top bunk jumped down so fast he almost broke his leg. But the Lord protected us from all harm and danger. I'll never forget the night I woke up and saw a huge white bulge trying to come in through the tent flap.

Suddenly, the counselor turned on his flashlight. We all sighed with relief when our "ghost" turned out to be a very curious cow. She thought our tent was a barn!

Our campsite was only a couple of blocks from the beach. We went swimming every day. The boys played soccer on the sand while the girls played dodge ball and other games. One day we had a greased watermelon fight in the water. The boys were divided into two teams, and whichever team managed to grab the watermelon and carry it out of the water got to eat it! Watermelon is my favorite fruit. It was such a hot day I decided I *had* to win. I nearly drowned in the process. The watermelon was so slippery that each time I dove down and got it, it would slip out of my arms before I could get it to the surface. It was a tough fight, but worth it. Somehow I got it up, and it was delicious!

Each evening we'd have a fun hour. We'd put on skits, laugh at all the funny things that had happened, and read from our daily camp newspaper. I even helped to write it.

After supper we'd walk down to the edge of a creek. We'd sit before a huge bonfire and think about all of our blessings. God seemed very close during those times. That's where I learned to really pray and listen to God. We'd worship there in the dark by the bonfire. The Lord talked to me very clearly. He told me I was a sinner, but He loved me. I asked Jesus to forgive my sins. From that moment on, life seemed different. God became real. His love and friendship seemed to surround me. The Bible verses we memorized began to make sense. I really enjoyed the Bible classes we had each morning.

I dreaded the last day of camp. I didn't want it to end. The whole week had been wonderful. God had been so real. I hated the thought of leaving this beautiful place and all the new friends I'd made.

At our last campfire, the pastor gave us a beautiful promise from God's Word. It was what Jesus had said to His disciples just before He left them to go up into heaven. Jesus said: "I am with you always, to the very end of the age" (Matthew 28:20*b*). As I rode the bus home, I kept repeating this promise to myself. It really is true! Jesus has been with me ever since!

4

A Very Different School

I must agree with Daniel. Camp was one of the most exciting experiences of my life. But March was just around the corner. March is the first month of autumn in Uruguay. Can you guess why I was excited? I was going to start in a new school!

Boys and girls in Uruguay go to school from March until November. Then they enjoy three months of sunshine and beaches during December, January, and February!

Once again I felt very lucky to be an MK in Uruguay. In most of South America, many children never learn to read or write. They don't have any schools near their homes. There are no laws to make children go to school. But Uruguay is famous because of its excellent schools. In Uruguay, by law, all children must go to school up to the sixth grade at least.

My friend Mabel went to the public school a block from my house. She went early in the morning. But by noon she was finished for the day. You see, the public schools here last only four hours a day. The children may choose to go in the morning, from eight o'clock to twelve o'clock, or, the sleepyheads can go in the afternoon, from one o'clock to five o'clock.

There are other differences too. All students must wear a uniform. Mabel wore a simple white tunic with a big navy blue bow tie. This is the standard uniform for all boys and girls in the public schools here. It is really a good rule, because then it doesn't matter whether you are rich or poor, or if your parents let you choose your own clothes or not. Everybody has to dress alike. Nobody feels ashamed of wearing the same old thing to school every day.

Maybe you'd like to move down to Uruguay to enjoy a shorter school day. If so, I must warn you that you must pass an examination on each subject. If you don't do well, you are not promoted to the next grade. It is very common to be 12 or 13 and still be in the sixth grade.

I did not attend the public school. Do you know why? My parents decided that I needed to learn to read and write in English as well as in Spanish. So they looked for a bilingual school, a school that teaches two languages. Since people from all over Europe have moved to live in Uruguay, there are bilingual schools for the British, French, Italian, German, and American children. These private schools last all day, because you have to learn twice as much. Each school has its own uniform.

My parents decided to send me to a bilingual Christian school. I like my uniform. I have a navy blue pleated skirt, a navy sweater, a white sailor's shirt and black sailor's tie, white socks, and black shoes. The boys wear pants, a sweater, and a plain white shirt without a tie. My shoes have to be polished every day.

Since my hair is long, I have to wear a headband or tie my hair up so it doesn't fall in my face.

My school day begins at 8:30 and I don't get out till 3:30 P.M. In the morning I have my Spanish classes: reading, writing, spelling, grammar, and math. In the afternoon I have the same subjects in English, except science instead of math.

I like my school. We have a beautiful chapel, a gym, an art room, a music class, and a roller skating rink. There is going to be a gym exhibition at the end of the year. There will be fancy costumes, lots of music, marching, exercises, and roller skating. I'm not too great at sports. But I really enjoy the variety of activities we learn in gym.

My school has an assembly once a week and Bible classes twice a week.

The only thing I don't like about school is the long bus ride back and forth. Mother says I really shouldn't complain. In many countries there are no bilingual schools in the cities where the missionaries live. Their children must go away to a boarding school (where the students live on campus). They only go home to visit their parents twice a year, during the holidays. I'm glad my school is only a half-hour ride away from home.

In the morning the ride is fun. The bus is usually empty, and I can sit down and enjoy the sights. But in the afternoon, the bus is full, and I have to stand most of the way. My book bag is heavy. I have a lot of homework, and I also carry a lunch box and gym bag. But I really can't feel too sorry for myself. Almost all the children in Uruguay travel the same way! Cars are very expensive here. Most families do not own a car. Everyone either walks, rides a bike, or rides the city bus.

After the long, bumpy ride home, I look forward to "taking milk." It is the custom in Uruguay to "take milk" around four or five in the afternoon. Usually, when the children get home from school, mother serves each one a big cup of tea, coffee, or hot chocolate. Actually, it's a cup of hot milk flavored with tea, coffee, or cocoa. Bread and butter and cookies are served with the hot milk. Everyone relaxes and enjoys the snack. On a cold winter afternoon, it's really a treat. Try it someday!

After "taking milk," I sit down to write out my spelling homework. My spelling list is twice as long as yours, because each word is in English and in Spanish, like this:

church   iglesia
house   casa
mother   mama

The accent mark in Spanish is very important. I have trouble remembering which words are accented and which aren't.

I usually have several math problems to work out and a history or geography lesson to memorize. Have you ever had to do that? I have to memorize the lesson, because the teacher might call on me tomorrow. If she does, I have to stand in front of the class and teach the lesson. I have to be able to tell the rest of the class all about the lesson, without looking at the book! Since I never know when it will be my turn, I have to study every day. So does everyone else. It really is hard, but I'm learning a lot!

If I finish my homework in time, I am allowed to watch cartoons on TV. Almost everyone in Uruguay has a television, but nobody watches it during the day. The TV stations don't start broadcasting until five in the afternoon. Most parents check to see that their children have finished their homework before they allow them to watch TV or go out to play with their friends.

If my spelling isn't done neatly, I have to rewrite it. If I can't tell my mother the lesson I have studied, I have to study it some more. Some days I have hardly any time to play. But I believe God wants me to be a good student. The Bible says: "Study to shew thyself approved unto God" (2 Timothy 2:15, KJV). And, "Whatever you do, work at it with all your heart, as working for the Lord" (Colossians 3:23). I want to witness for Jesus. Studying isn't easy, sometimes, but it is worth it!

I suppose you are wondering if I ever eat supper. In Uruguay, most parents work till 7 P.M., so supper is served after eight o'clock. Children eat supper, talk to their daddy, and then go to bed. On prayer meeting nights, supper is served *after* church.

It's just another one of those "opposite" things. When you eat supper, I take my snack (milk). When you have your bedtime snack, I eat supper.

5

Gauchos and Holidays

I was really surprised to learn that all schools close for a "Holy Week" sometime in March or April. You celebrate a holiday then too. Think for a minute! What is it?

Christians all around the world celebrate this special holy week. Let's see how well you remember. Can you match the days of the week with these special events in Jesus' life?

Choose from these days:

a. Palm Sunday   c. Friday   e. Easter Sunday
b. Thursday   d. Saturday

____ The day Jesus died on the Cross

____ The day Jesus rode into Jerusalem on a donkey. Everyone shouted praises to God and waved palm branches to honor Jesus as King.

____ The day Jesus ate the Last Supper with His disciples and washed their feet.

____ The day Jesus rose from the dead, giving us eternal life.

____ The Jewish Sabbath, when the disciples and friends of Jesus cried and believed Jesus would never come back to life.

You can check the answers on the bottom of the next page.

Very few boys and girls in Uruguay would be able to pass that quiz, even though they have the whole week off. Most Uruguayans call it Tourist Week, instead of Holy Week. It is similar to the Labor Day weekend in the United States. It is early in the fall and everyone tries to take a trip to visit relatives or go to the beach. Many people from Argentina and Brazil come to enjoy Uruguay's beaches.

Others call it "Semana Criolla" (say-MAH-nah cree-OH-yah). This means "the week of the cowboys." There are rodeos and a huge country fair. All of the prize cattle and sheep and horses are exhibited and judged. Uruguay is a cattle country. Our cowboys are called "gauchos" and dress differently from yours. They are easy to spot because of their baggy pants, boots, hats, and long heavy ponchos.

I wondered why they always carried a Thermos under their arm, until I tasted "mate" (MAH-tey). It is their own special tea. They drink it out of a gourd that is filled with green "mate" leaves. They are very tiny leaves ground almost to a powder. You add boiling water and suck the "mate" through a silver straw that has a strainer at the other end.

It reminds me of the American Indian's peace pipe, because a gaucho never drinks "mate" alone. He passes it around the circle from one friend to another. Nobody seems to worry about germs, even though they drink from the same straw. I guess they figure the hot water will kill all the germs.

When I drink "mate," I add sugar and let it cool a bit. It is really delicious that way.

One day a gaucho treated me to a delicious "torta frita" (TORE-tah FREE-tah) or "fried cake." It is flat,

Answers: (1) C; (2) A; (3) B; (4) E; (5) D

like a pancake, but deep-fried, like a doughnut. It is very easy to make and is a tasty treat. Next rainy day, try making some. Here is the recipe:

Torta Frita

Measure and sift together:
    2 cups flour
    1 teaspoon salt
    3 teaspoons baking powder

Melt in a saucepan: 1 tablespoon shortening. Mix together:

   the dry ingredients
   the hot melted shortening
   one-half cup of hot water

Knead the dough for about five minutes, and then make little balls the size of a Ping-Pong ball. Take one ball at a time and stretch it out with your fingers until it is about as thin and as big as a pancake. Poke a hole in the middle about the size of your little finger.

Do the same with all of the balls. Then deep-fry them in melted shortening or oil. Turn them over carefully when the edges begin to turn golden brown. Let them drain on a paper towel and cool before tasting them.

If you have a sweet tooth, like me, you may like to sprinkle sugar on them while they are still hot. This recipe makes about a dozen tortas.

There are no full-blooded Indians left in Uruguay. The Charruas (char-ROO-ahs) were a very fierce Indian tribe. They fought against the early colonists in a life-or-death struggle to keep the land. They refused to share the land. So they either died in battle or fled across the river into Argentina or Paraguay.

One of their weapons, however, has remained a tradition among the gauchos. It is called a "bolas." It is made of three long ropes tied together. There is a heavy stone ball at the end of each rope. The gaucho uses these to hunt "nandu," a bird similar to a small ostrich. The gaucho chases the bird on horseback. He swings the "bolas" above his head like a lasso. Then he lets go of them. If he aims right, the three ropes wind around the bird's long legs. Then the gaucho has a chance to catch it.

Fancy decorated hollow chocolate Easter eggs are the only reminder that Jesus' tomb is empty. Do you remember how surprised Mary was to find an empty tomb? Well, you'd be surprised, too, if you got a Uruguayan Easter egg. Inside the hollow chocolate egg there is always a surprise gift.

My Uruguayan friends have never heard of the Easter Bunny. They don't decorate hard-boiled eggs or have an Easter parade. Those are all spring customs, and Easter comes in the fall in Uruguay.

However, in September, all of the boys and girls celebrate another week-long holiday. Then they have parades, make paper flowers, choose queens, and have kite-flying contests. Can you guess why? It's spring vacation!

It was hard to get used to going to school in June. But the weather is so cold, it doesn't seem like a good time for the summer holidays. Instead, I get two weeks off school in July, for winter holidays. In the evenings I love to curl up in the armchair by the fire and read my favorite books. I love to read. But even before I learned how, I already had a favorite book, the Bible. My mother would read to me from it every day. It's full of all kinds of stories. Here are a few clues about some of my favorite Bible story heroes. See if you recognize them.

1. I am a man in the Old Testament. I had 11 brothers and was my father's favorite. He gave me a coat of many colors and made my brothers jealous. They sold me as a slave. But God blessed me and later used me to keep my family from starving. I became a ruler in Egypt. Who am I?
2. I am a prince in the Old Testament. I was tak-

en prisoner to a faraway country where everyone was ordered to worship an idol. I was thrown into a den of lions for praying to God. But He protected me. I showed the king that there is only one true, living God. Who am I?
3. I am a lady in the Old Testament. I was raised in a country that worshiped idols. But when I grew up I married a man that worshiped God. When he died, I went to Israel and lived among God's people. God blessed me with many new friends, a new husband, and a baby boy. My great-grandson became the famous King David. Who am I? *(See bottom of page for answers.)*

Every day my family reads the Bible and prays together. One of my dad's favorite Bible verses is: "Don't worry about anything; instead, pray about everything; tell God your needs and don't forget to thank him for his answers" (Philippians 4:6, TLB).

So we pray about everything. We pray for a sunny day so we can go to the park for a picnic. We pray for the Lord to help us find a pair of new school shoes that won't be too expensive. When we get lonely, we pray for the mail to get through. Then we can read letters from my grandma and our friends back in the United States and Canada. I always pray that my friends at school will come to know Jesus as their Savior. We pray for missionaries all over the world. We pray especially for the people who live in countries where it is against the law to read the Bible and pray. Do you remember to pray for missionaries and believers in other countries?

(1) Joseph; (2) Daniel; (3) Ruth

6

My Favorite Holiday: Christmas

Christmas is my favorite holiday. In Uruguay it is extraspecial! School ends the second week in December. My long summer holidays get off to a super start with Vacation Bible School. Christmas season is a great time for VBS. At recess we go to the park and play games, skip rope, or relax in the shade of the trees. Each day a different church family provides the snack. On Saturday, we each bring our own picnic lunch and spend the day at the beach.

Craft time is really exciting. For a couple of days we make paper chains and decorations for the church Christmas tree. Then we make manger scenes to take home. I love making surprise gifts for my parents. Vacation Bible School is the perfect place to make Christmas presents. In our music class we learn carols and special songs for our church Christmas program. We also practice our poems and plays.

Most of the families in my neighborhood never go to church. Some send their children to Sunday School, but almost all of them send their kids to Bible school. Some even come to our Christmas program.

We all work very hard to put on an extraspecial Christmas program. It will probably be the only religious service many of our neighbors will attend all year. Everyone celebrates Christmas, but very few remember it is Jesus' birthday. At VBS we remind the whole neighborhood that God loves us and sent His Son, Jesus. The church Christmas program is the largest community affair of the whole season!

Since it is hot, we usually build a platform outside and have the program at night. The colored lights and music usually attract many people who would never walk into the church. I'm happy to think I had a special part in putting Christ into my neighbor's Christmas.

At the end of the program each child receives a bag of cookies, candy, and popcorn. It's the church's way of saying "Feliz Navidad" (fay-LEES nah-vee-THAHTH)—"Merry Christmas!"

Boys and girls in Uruguay celebrate Christmas in different ways. This year I got to help Nelson, my next-door neighbor, make a Judas. I made the face out of an old throw cushion and got a torn shirt from Dad to stuff. Nelson had a ragged pair of jeans and a straw hat. Between the two of us, we made a pretty neat-looking dummy. In the evenings we sat out on the sidewalk and asked people to give us a "penny for Judas." We used the money to buy firecrackers and shooting stars to set off at midnight on Christmas Eve.

The Bible says that the skies were lighted by a choir of angels on the first Christmas. But in Uruguay, the skies are ablaze with fireworks. Shouts of "Feliz Navidad" ring through the night.

The traditional Christmas dinner is a very late-night cookout on Christmas Eve. Instead of turkey, we charcoal-broil beef, lamb, or pork. I like the lamb best.

Since it's summer, we don't eat hot vegetables and stuffing. Instead, Mother makes potato salad and serves a fresh garden salad. This year I'm going to help make the traditional fruit salad for dessert.

Instead of cookies, we eat "pan dulce," a special cake full of glazed fruit and nuts. While supper is cooking (the meat usually takes about three hours to cook), we visit our neighbors and wish them a Merry Christmas. At each house I'm usually offered a glass of Coke and a piece of "pan dulce." But I prefer the nuts and "turron" (too-RRON), a caramel candy bar full of nuts that is sold at Christmastime. Christmas Eve is a noisy, neighborly, friendly evening of sharing, eating, and peeking under the tree.

My first Christmas, I was very disappointed when I saw Nelson's tree. It was a little, two-foot tree on a coffee table. I figured only three or four presents would fit under it, and I was right. You see, most people here don't exchange big gifts for Christmas. Usually each child receives one small package, such as a toy car or a pair of sunglasses. Christmas is a time of sharing good food and friendship. We children especially enjoy playing hide-and-seek in the dark, burning our Judases, and scaring everyone with firecrackers. Nobody goes to bed before two or three o'clock in the morning.

Christmas Day is usually spent at the beach. Since Montevideo is surrounded by water, it's only about three or four miles to a beach. It's the perfect place to try out new presents and eat leftovers.

Do you remember the Christmas story in the Bible?

Can you remember who gave Jesus presents? According to tradition, the three wise men didn't arrive on Christmas Day. They came from a far country in the East and followed the star for many days and nights. They even went to the palace in Jerusalem first, to seek the newborn King. So they didn't get to Bethlehem until January 6. Children in Uruguay celebrate King's Day on January 6.

I have been a good girl most of the year—and since I studied very hard and was promoted with an excellent grade, I am hoping the three wise men will each bring me a special gift this King's Day. I wrote them a letter the first week in December, telling them I wanted a new bathing suit, a children's Bible, and a new pair of roller skates with red sneakers. Now all I can do is wait and see if I get them.

Last year I followed Nelson's advice and left a pile of hay and a huge pan of water beside the front door. This was so the camels could enjoy themselves while the kings unloaded my gifts. Instead of hanging a stocking by the fireplace, I put my biggest pair of shoes outside my bedroom door to be filled with gifts. I had a hard time sleeping January 5. When I woke up, the water and hay were gone and my shoes contained my three wishes.

Christmas is definitely my favorite holiday. I love Jesus, and I love celebrating His birthday. I think it's great that everyone receives gifts on Jesus' birthday, don't you? In Uruguay, it is a happy birthday and quite a long celebration too. It's the only birthday party I know of that lasts two whole weeks and to which everyone is invited!

Happy birthday, Jesus! Thank You for all the joy You bring to everyone, all over the world!

Postscript

I'm not a little girl anymore. I grew up and returned to the United States to finish high school. Then I attended Olivet Nazarene College. I became an elementary school teacher and taught in Darby, Pennsylvania, for three years. Then I returned to Uruguay.

There I fell in love and married one of my childhood friends, Daniel Gonzalez. He is the same Daniel that told you about camp. He's been to over 20 camps since then! He grew up in Uruguay and became a minister.

Guess where we pastored? The Carrasco Church of the Nazarene. It is the very same church we grew up in. My dad was the pastor there.

My sister, Beverly, married Daniel's brother, Eduardo. They pastored a Church of the Nazarene in Ecuador, South America.

Daniel and I have two daughters, Cristina and Karina. They think that Uruguay is wonderful.

My friend Mabel grew up and was baptized. She was given her first Sunday School class to teach when she was only 13. She married a Nazarene minister and became the district superintendent's wife! She and her husband, Rev. Walter Rodriguez, traveled to the General Assembly in Kansas City in 1980. Her dream of traveling to the United States came true!

We have all shared God's message of love with the people of Uruguay. He has really blessed all of us.